Blastoff! Readers are carefully developed by literacy experts to build reading stamina and move students toward fluency by combining standards-based content with developmentally appropriate text.

 Level 1 provides the most support through repetition of high-frequency words, light text, predictable sentence patterns, and strong visual support.

 Level 2 offers early readers a bit more challenge through varied sentences, increased text load, and text-supportive special features.

 Level 3 advances early-fluent readers toward fluency through increased text load, less reliance on photos, advancing concepts, longer sentences, and more complex special features.

★ **Blastoff! Universe**

 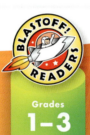 

This edition first published in 2026 by Bellwether Media, Inc.

No part of this publication may be reproduced in whole or in part without written permission of the publisher. For information regarding permission, write to Bellwether Media, Inc., Attention: Permissions Department, 3500 American Blvd W, Suite 150, Bloomington, MN 55431.

Library of Congress Cataloging-in-Publication Data

LC record for Ducks available at: https://lccn.loc.gov/2025012863

Text copyright © 2026 by Bellwether Media, Inc. BLASTOFF! READERS and associated logos are trademarks and/or registered trademarks of Bellwether Media, Inc. Bellwether Media is a division of FlutterBee Education Group.

Editor: Betsy Rathburn   Designer: Gabriel Hilger

Printed in the United States of America, North Mankato, MN.

Table of Contents

What Are Ducks? 4
Ducks in the City 10
Ducks and People 18
Glossary 22
To Learn More 23
Index 24

What Are Ducks?

Ducks are birds that live near water. Many ducks live in cities.

Common City Duck

mallard

Duck **feathers** are **waterproof**. Males often have more colorful feathers than females.

Ducks have **webbed feet**. These help them swim and dive.

Ducks in the City

Ducks often live in parks. They make nests in bushes and tall grass.

Duck Homes

bushes

tall grass

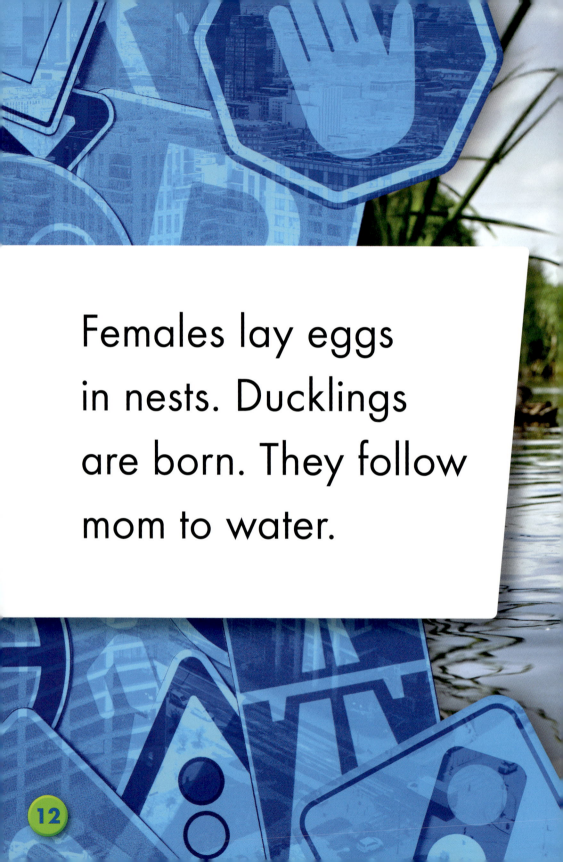

Females lay eggs in nests. Ducklings are born. They follow mom to water.

Ducks swim in **fountains** and ponds. They find food underwater. They eat fish, bugs, and plants.

fountain

Duck Food

fish bugs plants

15

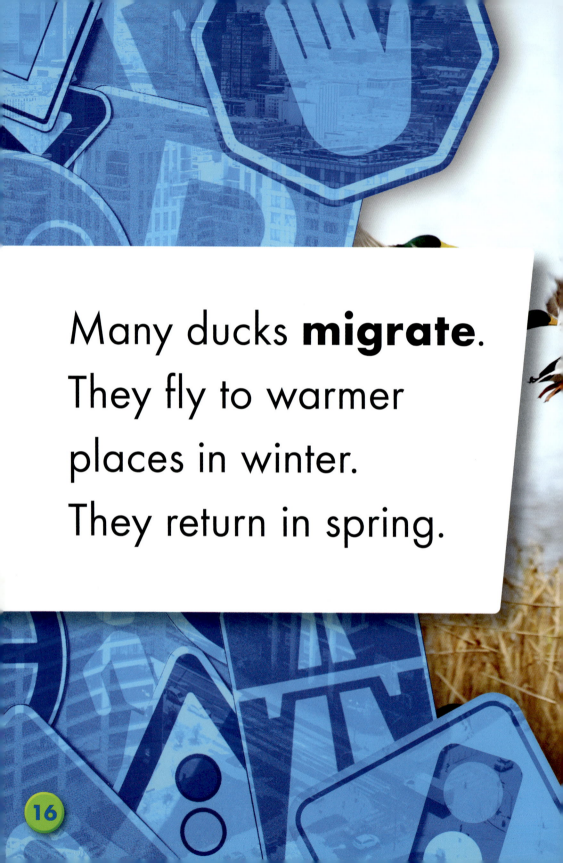

Many ducks **migrate**. They fly to warmer places in winter. They return in spring.

migrating

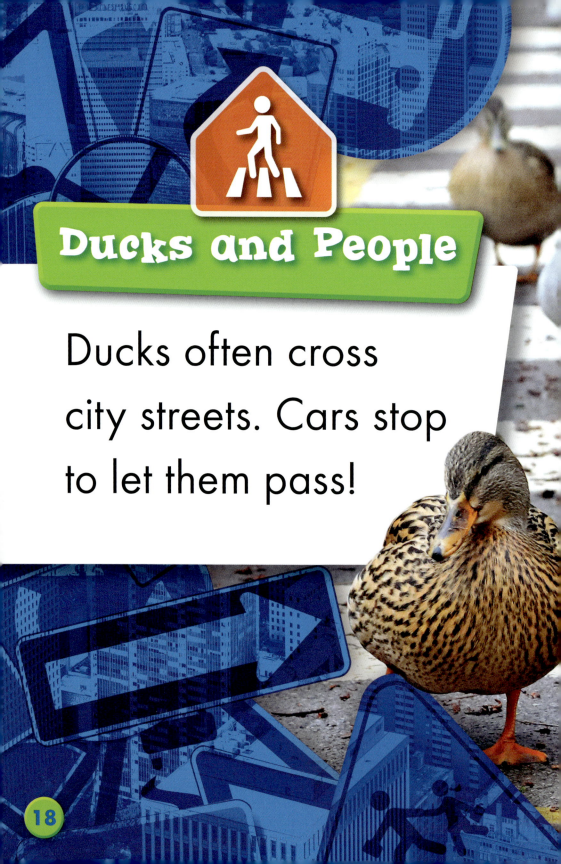

Ducks and People

Ducks often cross city streets. Cars stop to let them pass!

People watch ducks in city parks. They hear ducks quack!

Glossary

feathers

light, soft coverings on birds' bodies

waterproof
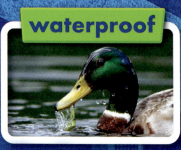
able to keep water from passing through

fountains
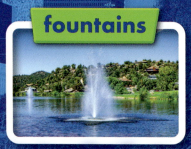
structures that shoot out water

webbed feet

feet that have thin skin between the toes

migrate

to travel from one place to another, often with the seasons

To Learn More

AT THE LIBRARY

Deniston, Natalie. *Goose or Duck?* Minneapolis, Minn.: Jump!, 2025.

Leaf, Christina. *Baby Chicken or Baby Duck?* Minneapolis, Minn.: Bellwether Media, 2025.

Riggs, Kate. *Ducks.* Mankato, Minn.: Creative Education, 2026.

ON THE WEB

FACTSURFER

Factsurfer.com gives you a safe, fun way to find more information.

1. Go to www.factsurfer.com.
2. Enter "ducks" into the search box and click 🔍.
3. Select your book cover to see a list of related content.

Index

birds, 4
bushes, 10
cities, 4, 18, 20
common city
 duck, 5
dive, 8, 9
ducklings, 12, 13
eggs, 12
feathers, 6
females, 6, 7, 12
fly, 16
food, 14, 15
fountains, 14, 15
grass, 10
homes, 11
males, 6, 7
migrate, 16, 17

nests, 10, 12, 13
parks, 10, 20
people, 20
ponds, 14
quack, 20
spring, 16
streets, 18
swim, 8, 14
water, 4, 12, 14
waterproof, 6
webbed feet, 8, 9
winter, 16

The images in this book are reproduced through the courtesy of: Oleksandr Lytvynenko, front cover (duck); lunamarina, front cover (city); BigGabig, p. 3; Andrey, pp. 4-5; shishiga, p. 5 (mallard); rck, pp. 6-7; Mark, pp. 8-9; Pete, p. 9 (webbed feet); kozorog, pp. 10-11; lissart, p. 11 (bushes); Andi111, p. 11 (tall grass); tygrys74, pp. 12-13; fotoparus, p. 13 (nest); Viktoria, pp. 14-15; Rostislav, p. 15 (fish); alohapatty, p. 15 (bugs); Denny, p. 15 (plants); Creaturart Images, pp. 16-17; Judith, pp. 18-19; Max Topchii, pp. 20-21; matushaban, p. 22 (feathers); Scott Bufkin, p. 22 (fountains); Ihi, p. 22 (migrate); tomatito26, p. 22 (waterproof); LoweStock, p. 22 (webbed).